"Don't ruin a good day by worrying about what **might** happen tomorrow."

"interviews"

An Interview with
jim plunkett

By Larry Batson
Photographs by Vernon J. Biever

CREATIVE EDUCATION/CHILDRENS PRESS

Published by Creative Educational Society, Inc., 123 South Broad Street,
Mankato, Minnesota 56001. Copyright © 1977 by Creative Educational
Society, Inc. International copyrights reserved in all countries. No part of
this book may be reproduced in any form without written permission from
the publisher. Printed in the United States.

Library of Congress Cataloging in Publication Data

Batson, Larry, 1930-   Jim Plunkett.

  1. Plunkett, Jim—Juvenile literature.
2. Quarterback (Football)—Biography—Juvenile literature. I. Title.
GV939.P63B37   796.33'2'0924 [B]   76-27640
ISBN 0-87191-570-7

There are people who rush frantically through life, always seeking something better or different or more exciting. But not Jim Plunkett.

Plunkett embraces life. He accepts whatever each day brings. He enjoys the good times and endures the bad ones. He knows that neither will last forever.

"Enjoy what you've got while it's there," the San Francisco 49ers' quarterback says. "Don't ruin a good day by worrying about what might happen tomorrow. And when you're having a rough day, keep plugging. Things will turn around."

Plunkett never seems to be in a hurry. He'll leave a stadium after a football game and find a crowd of kids waiting beside his car.

He'll sit on the fender and spend an hour with them. He'll sign autographs and explain why he called a certain play that day. He'll show them how he grips a ball to pass it or how he hands off the ball to a runner.

When all the autographs are signed and all the questions are answered, Plunkett will thank the kids for coming to see him. "It was real nice of you," he'll say. "I enjoyed it."

Then he'll probably go out to dinner. Sometimes it will be a big meal at an expensive restaurant where famous and wealthy people will flock around him.

More often it will be a smaller, quieter place where he will meet two or three friends and talk quietly.

Some nights Plunkett will go straight home to soak in a hot bath and rest. He's always tired and hurting after a football game. As a quarterback, he is the key to his team's offense. That makes him the No. 1 target of opponents. They hit him hard every chance they get.

Plunkett is one of the new breed of quarterbacks who are replacing the older stars of professional football. He is a fine passer and highly intelligent, a player who can call his own plays and detect weaknesses in opponents' defenses. But he is also big enough and fast enough and strong enough to run with the football, too. He can hold off a rusher with a stiff-arm or run right over a tackler — and often does.

Plunkett enjoys playing football tremendously. But he knows that football and fame and the big salary can't last forever. And he doesn't need them to be happy. He always has known that there are more important things in life.

"Right now I'm lucky to be playing football and I enjoy it very much. It's challenging and stimulating. I can make a good deal of money and that's nice, too. Not that I ever thought I had to have a lot of money to be happy.

"There are lots of people who are terribly poor. I'm sorry for them and I think they should be helped to get on their feet, to find jobs and all that.

"But there are people who think so much about money that they can't be happy with just enough of it. With people like that, poverty is a state of mind."

Plunkett is an orderly, precise person. When he is talking with someone, he listens carefully. Then he pauses to get his thoughts straight before he answers. He doesn't like to skip around from one topic to another. He'd rather finish one, then move on.

"Actually, if
I hadn't become
a pro athlete,
I suppose I'd have
been a
teacher
or a
social worker
or
maybe a
lawyer."

"I don't really like putting labels on people," he said. "That's like putting them in boxes and saying that they have to behave a certain way because they belong in a certain box.

"I know that's not true. I've been around enough to know that all people have a lot in common no matter where they come from or what color their skin is or what church they go to. It's all right to be proud of all those things. I'm not saying it isn't. But it's wrong to think that they make you any better or any worse than someone else.

"Take me, for instance. I'm an athlete and my folks didn't have much money. Some people put me in their box labeled 'Poor Jocks'. They think that all I must care about is playing games and making money. They don't know me, but they think they know all about people like me.

"Actually, if I hadn't become a pro athlete, I suppose I'd have been a teacher or a social worker or maybe a lawyer. I might have got into politics by now. I was interested in all those things. I still am.

"But I had to make a choice. Some day, when the football is over, I might go into one of those other things. Or I might find something else that interests me more. Then I suppose the people who have to label everybody else will have to find a new box to put me in.

"I don't like to have people think of me as somebody who overcame special problems. That's kind of like putting my parents down. They were very supportive, very good to me.

"Both my dad and mom were blind," he said, "but I never thought of that as a problem. It was just the way things were at home. They were just like other parents. I never thought of them as being handicapped.

"They met and married in New Mexico (at a school for the blind)," Plunkett said. "They moved to California from there and I was born in San Jose (on December 5, 1947).

"My father had a newsstand. I always had jobs, like at a grocery store and a gas station. I sold papers, too. I never felt deprived. We had a happy life."

14

The name Plunkett is Irish, but he is often referred to as a Chicano, meaning a Mexican-American. How about that? he was asked.

"I'm about 90 percent Mexican with some Irish and German mixed up in there," he said. "Sometimes people call me a Chicano and that's all right by me. I don't use the word very often myself, maybe because I don't speak Spanish.

"If I had to describe myself, I'd say I was an American, a Californian, and a ball player."

Whatever Plunkett decides to do when he's no longer a ball-player, he's almost certain to do it in the area where he was born, grew up, and returned to play as a pro football star. He loves the area and asked to be traded to the San Francisco 49ers after the 1975 pro season, his fifth with the New England Patriots.

"I like to travel," he said, "especially driving. But I always come home. I built a house here. I like to see my old friends, my family and the familiar sights I grew up with.

"My father died in 1969 and my two sisters are married. But my mother lives with me. And our family is still close. We talk a lot and visit each other when we can."

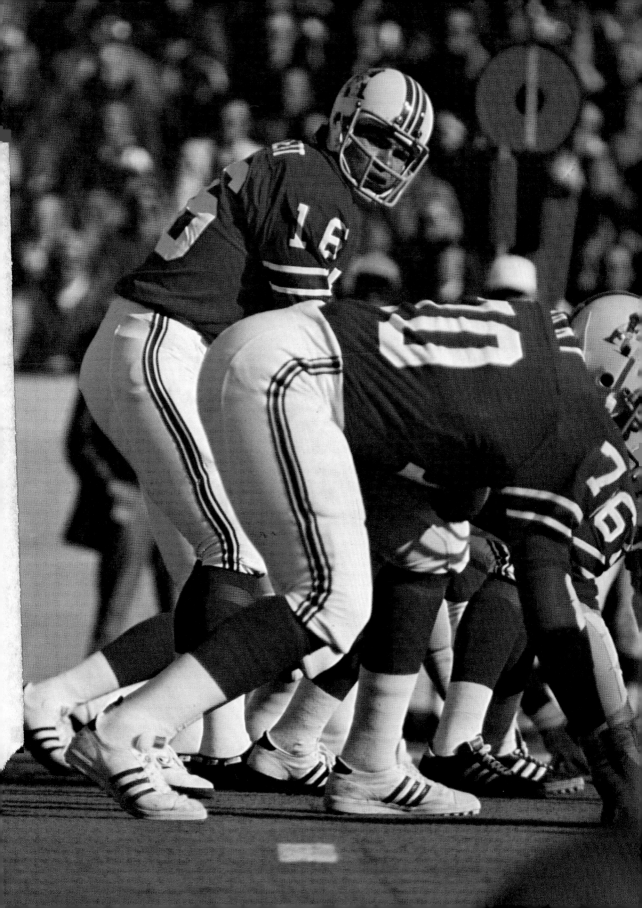

San Jose is a pleasant, prosperous city of about 450,000 population. It is located in northern California, inland from San Francisco. There is a fertile farming valley there. Grassy hills border the valley and there are mountains less than an hour's drive away to the north and east.

"I don't know if there is any place anywhere else in the world that has the variety that we have here in the Bay Area," Plunkett said. "I never get tired of it."

"Both my dad and mom were **blind,**

Once the region around San Jose was all farm and ranch land, but now communities have been built all over the Bay Area. The climate is pleasant, not as hot as in Southern California, but seldom is there any really cold weather. Snow is extremely rare, except in the mountains.

If he doesn't feel like driving, Plunkett can take a train from San Jose to San Francisco. They are shining, steel, electric trains that zip along at 70 miles an hour. When they reach the bay across from San Francisco, the trains dip into tunnels that run under the ocean. Then they emerge in the city and stop at places like Fisherman's Wharf; Powell Street, where the cable cars turn around; and the waterfront, where ships from all over the world are anchored.

but I
never
thought of it as a problem."

There is Chinatown in downtown San Francisco. Plunkett can walk through a carved wooden gate guarded by stone lions and wander for hours among Oriental shops, restaurants, and homes.

If he stays on the train, it will cross another branch of the bay to the peninsula that juts into the Pacific

Ocean. The city of Palo Alto is there and so is the campus of Stanford University where Plunkett went to college.

Plunkett could have gone to any college in the country. His grades were good enough and his athletic ability was that impressive. But he chose Stanford "because it was close to home."

When Jim was 14 he passed a football 63 yards in a contest. That's farther than some professional quarterbacks can throw one. He quarterbacked the James Like High School team to two championships and met John Ralston, then coach of Stanford, at a high school all-star game.

Jim had been involved in sports since the fifth grade. "I played football, basketball, and baseball," he said. "Wrestled, too, and did most everything on the track team. It was hard for me to decide on a favorite sport.

"I was always busy as a kid," Plunkett said, "always moving around and doing something. There was so much to see and investigate that it was impossible not to be interested. That set the pattern for my life, I guess. I'm that way now.

"I played an awful lot of baseball — pitched, caught, played every position, I think. I seriously considered a career in professional baseball. But I guess I loved football just a little bit more."

Jim was a good student, not a genius but far above average in intelligence. He graduated from high school with a B-plus average and was a B student at Stanford.

He had an outstanding record at Stanford, but it didn't start that way. For a time, there was doubt that he would play at all. Then for a while, there was talk of switching him from quarterback to another position.

"In a physical checkup just before I started college, they found a tumor on my thyroid gland," he said. "We were afraid it was cancerous, but it turned out not to be. Really scared me, though.

"After I got squared away physically, I messed up in the classroom. I had trouble adjusting to college, as a lot of students do. But I switched my major to political science, which really interested me, and I got straightened out there, too. I did all right after that. I finished with a B average or a little better.

"Then Coach Ralston asked me if I'd be willing to switch positions. I'd played defensive end in that all-star game he coached because our squad, the Northern California team, had several outstanding quarterbacks but was weak at end. I didn't care much for the idea, but I said I'd think it over."

That summer Plunkett practiced almost every day with kids from his former high school. Some days he threw hundreds of passes. When practice opened at Stanford in the fall, he told Coach Ralston that he wanted to stay at quarterback.

"Practicing with the kids became a habit, too," he said. "I still do it. I read in the papers and magazines that I work with them. It sounds as if I'm doing social work.

"It's not that way. It's nothing formal. We're friends and we just have fun together. We shoot baskets and they act as my receivers when I want to practice passing. We talk a lot and fool around. I enjoy it."

Later on, when Plunkett had the opportunity to turn professional after his junior year at Stanford, those friends back at the high school were one of the reasons he decided to stay in college.

"I don't really like putting labels on people."

"I was red-shirted my sophomore year," he said. "The coach held me out of games, so I had a year of eligibility left after my original college class graduated. But I decided to stay in school.

"There were several reasons. I wanted my degree, for one thing. A professional athlete never knows when his career will end. I'd already had one knee operation.

"Then we had almost got into the Rose Bowl my junior season and we all wanted to give it one more shot. I also was close to my teammates and didn't want to leave them.

"Then there were the kids in high school. I'd spent a lot of time talking some of them out of quitting school. How could I tell them to stay in high school and turn around and quit college myself? No way."

Plunkett went on to set national passing records in 1970 during his last season at Stanford. The Indians won the Pacific Coast Conference championship and defeated Ohio State in the Rose Bowl. Plunkett completed 20 passes in that game and was named its most valuable player. Several key passes were thrown to Randy Vataha,

Plunkett's closest friend on the team and later a teammate on the New England Patriots.

"I helped recruit Randy for Stanford," Plunkett said, laughing. "My coach sent me to meet him at the airport and show him around the campus.

"I'd been hearing stories about this great receiver from junior college and I was expecting to see some big stud with hands like scoop shovels.

"But Randy isn't very tall — about 5-feet, 10–inches, I guess. If I hadn't been wearing my letter sweater, I doubt that we'd have gotten together. He spotted me and came over and introduced himself. I wondered if those stories about his ability could be true, but he soon showed us that he was big enough to do anything he had to on a football field. He's very tough and quick and he can catch anything he can reach. He can outjump most taller players, too.

"We kid him a lot, though. He worked one summer at Disneyland playing Bashful, one of the Seven Dwarfs. The story we put out is that he's the only retired dwarf in pro football. But as I say, he's plenty big enough."

"...turn around and quit college myself? No way."

Football writers often exaggerate reports of Plunkett's size and strength. For instance, it has been reported often that he is 6-feet, 4-inches and can throw a football more than 100 yards.

"I'm a little bit over 6-feet, 2-inches and I weigh 212 pounds," he said. "I don't know why people stretch those things.

"I feel comfortable throwing a ball around 60 yards and I have thrown a pass 70 yards in the air. Lots of people have done that.

"I don't know how far I could throw if I tried simply for distance. That has nothing to do with being a good passer. Accuracy and timing are the important things."

"You earn respect by

being
consistent..."

There is also more than passing involved in becoming a professional quarterback. For instance, the intangible quality of leadership. Plunkett has that quality.

Don Shula, coach of the Miami Dolphins, rates him as a quarterback who can lift an average team to greatness by his own example and performance.

Bud Grant, coach of the Minnesota Vikings, says, "Some guys are just winners. There are people in the league who can throw the ball harder or more accurately. There are quarterbacks who have been around longer and can call plays a little better, maybe. But Plunkett is one of the winners."

Alan Page, defensive tackle of the Vikings, agrees with Grant. "One word comes to mind when I think of Plunkett," Page said. "That's determination. He will not quit. He never seems to think that he is beaten."

The San Francisco 49ers valued his athletic and leadership abilities so much that in April 1976 they gave up a young quarterback plus three first-round and one second-round draft choices to bring him back to the Bay Area.

Plunkett says that leadership is hard to describe. ''People lead in different ways,'' he explained. ''There are quiet leaders who do it by example. There are inspirational types.''

''You have to do the job on the field, but that's not the only thing involved. Some really excellent passers aren't leaders. And there are quarterbacks in the league who are fine leaders, but don't have nearly as much physical ability as others.

''I guess leading really means that a team acquires confidence in you. And that starts by your having confidence in yourself. You earn respect by being consistent in performance and behavior. You have to control yourself.

''You have to keep plugging away,'' he added. ''It may sound corny, but it's true. You can't quit on yourself or your team.''

creative education

"interviews"